Zoom in on the
NATIONAL ANTHEM

ZOOM in
on American
Symbols

Cecelia H. Brannon

Enslow Publishing

101 W. 23rd Street
Suite 240
New York, NY 10011
USA

enslow.com

WORDS TO KNOW

anthem A patriotic song used by a country.

ceremony A formal gathering to celebrate an occasion.

garrison A group of soldiers who live in a fort to protect it.

harbor A place on the coast where many ships dock.

inspire To encourage someone to make or do something.

lyrics The words to a song.

melody The notes of a song.

verse A part of a poem or song.

CONTENTS

1   The War of 1812 . . . . **5**

2   "What So Proudly We Hailed" **8**

3   Who Was Francis Scott Key? **12**

4   The National Anthem **16**

"The Star-Spangled Banner"
Lyrics **21**

Activity: Write Your Own
Anthem **22**

Learn More **24**

Index **24**

This painting shows the burning of buildings in Washington, DC, during the War of 1812.

The War of 1812

Just thirty-three years after America separated from Britain and became a new nation, the United States went to war with Britain again. The war began over fights about land and became heated very fast. On August 24, 1814, British troops set fire to the Capitol building and the White House in Washington, DC. The American people were worried about the future of their nation.

The Battle of Baltimore

On September 13, 1814, British troops began firing on Fort McHenry in the harbor of Baltimore. The bombing lasted twenty-five hours. Ships were destroyed. Between 1,500 and 1,800 bombs were

Fort McHenry

Built in 1798, Fort McHenry is a star-shaped fort built in Baltimore Harbor. It is named after James McHenry, a signer of the United States Constitution and secretary of war under Presidents Washington and Adams.

fired at the fort. But as the shots stopped firing, the smoke cleared, the sun rose, and a large American flag was raised above the fort. The sight of the stars and stripes inspired one of the most famous poems in American history.

Fort McHenry

Meanwhile, in the Harbor...

Lawyer Francis Scott Key was on a British ship, working for the release of an American, when the battle at Fort McHenry began. For safety, he stayed on the ship several miles out into the harbor. He could only watch in horror as the fort was hit by rockets and bombs. But as dawn broke, and he saw the flag waving above the fort, he knew that the Americans had won the battle. Right away he began writing the poem that would one day become the country's national anthem.

"What So Proudly We Hailed"

The flag that flew above Fort McHenry is now a national treasure. It is called the Star-Spangled Banner because it inspired the lyrics to the famous song. It is a large garrison flag, meaning that it is bigger than most flags. That flag is not the same as the flag we use today. Because the nation was still new, there were only fifteen stars on the flag that inspired Francis Scott Key.

Francis Scott Key waves his hat at the flag flying after the 1814 battle in Baltimore Harbor.

The Flag Makers

The flag at Fort McHenry was sewn by hand by a widow named Mary Pickersgill. George Armistad, the commander of the fort, asked Pickersgill to sew the flag in 1813. It took her seven weeks. She had the help of her teenage daughters, Eliza and Mary Young, and a servant, Grace Wisher, who was thirteen.

Still on Display

If you'd like to see the Star-Spangled Banner, you can! It has been on display at the Smithsonian Museum of American History Washington, DC, since 1907. It is kept in a special case under temperature control and low lighting to help preserve the fragile fabric.

The original Star-Spangled Banner was 30 feet (9 meters) tall and 42 feet (12 meters) wide.

Who Was Francis Scott Key?

Francis Scott Key (known as "Frank" to family and friends) was born on August 1, 1779, in Maryland. His grandparents had come to America from England in 1726. His father served as a captain during the Revolutionary War.

Frank attended St. John's College in Annapolis, Maryland, and became a lawyer in Baltimore. He and his wife, Mary Tayloe Lloyd, had eleven children.

Francis Scott Key was a distant cousin of the famous writer F. Scott Fitzgerald, who was named after him.

More Than a Poet

From 1833 to 1841, Key was the United States district attorney for the District of Columbia. His most famous case was against Richard Lawrence, who tried and failed to kill President Andrew Jackson.

Key enjoyed writing poetry. Most of his poems were religious,

The First Title

Francis Scott Key's poem was originally titled "The Defence of Fort M'Henry." It became "The Star-Spangled Banner" a few months later when stores started selling it as sheet music.

but his most famous poem is patriotic. He began writing it on the back of a letter while still on the ship in Baltimore Harbor. He rushed home to Washington, DC, and continued to write the poem. When finished, it was four verses long. Only the first verse is used as the national anthem, but the entire poem is often read during public ceremonies.

The Francis Scott Key Bridge in Baltimore stands on the spot from where the British fired on Fort McHenry.

The National Anthem

The poem written by Francis Scott Key did not have a melody at first. It was simply a poem. But when Key gave a copy of his poem to Judge Joseph H. Nicholson, the judge noticed that the words fit perfectly with a popular English song, "The Anacreontic Song" by composer John Stafford Smith. Key's poem was then set to music.

The cover of the sheet music for the national anthem

A Patriotic Song

During the US Civil War, the song was a comfort to many Americans. It became more popular over the years, and by the 1890s, the military used the song whenever it raised or lowered the flag. "The Star-Spangled Banner" was played during the first game of the 1918 World Series, which began the tradition of the song being played before every game.

The song did not officially become the anthem of the United States until 1931, when John Phillip Sousa, the famous American march composer, argued that the song would make a perfect anthem. On March 3, 1931, President Herbert Hoover declared the song the national anthem of the United States.

The US Flag Code states that whenever the anthem is played and the flag is displayed, every person present, except those in uniform, must stand at attention facing the flag with the right hand over the heart. Members of the military must salute, and hats should be removed as a sign of respect. The song has

Super Anthem

Many famous American singers have performed "The Star-Spangled Banner," especially before the Super Bowl every year, watched by millions of people across the country. Whitney Houston, Beyoncé, Christina Aguilera, Idina Menzel, and Lady Gaga have all been given the honor.

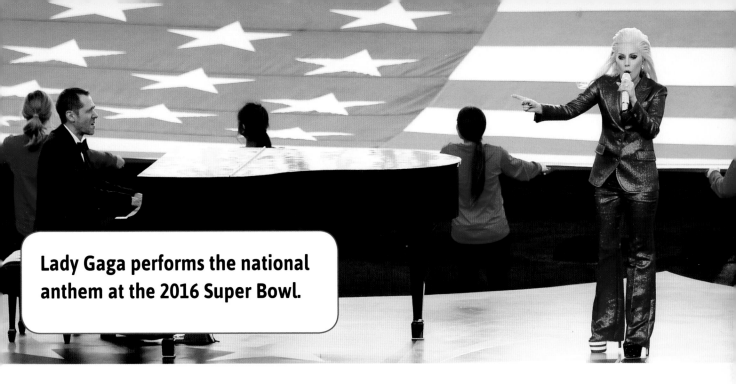

Lady Gaga performs the national anthem at the 2016 Super Bowl.

been translated into many languages, including German, Hebrew, Spanish, Yiddish, French, Samoan, and Navajo, reflecting the many different people who come together to make the United States the nation that it is today.

The Star-Spangled Banner

O say can you see, by the dawn's early light,
What so proudly we hailed at the twilight's last gleaming,
Whose broad stripes and bright stars through the perilous fight,
O'er the ramparts we watched, were so gallantly streaming?
And the rockets' red glare, the bombs bursting in air,
Gave proof through the night that our flag was still there;
O say does that star-spangled banner yet wave
O'er the land of the free and the home of the brave?

On the shore dimly seen through the mists of the deep,
Where the foe's haughty host in dread silence reposes,
What is that which the breeze, o'er the towering steep,
As it fitfully blows, half conceals, half discloses?
Now it catches the gleam of the morning's first beam,
In full glory reflected now shines in the stream:
'Tis the star-spangled banner, O! long may it wave
O'er the land of the free and the home of the brave.

And where is that band who so vauntingly swore
That the havoc of war and the battle's confusion,
A home and a country, should leave us no more?
Their blood has washed out their foul footsteps' pollution.
No refuge could save the hireling and slave
From the terror of flight, or the gloom of the grave:
And the star-spangled banner in triumph doth wave,
O'er the land of the free and the home of the brave.

O thus be it ever, when freemen shall stand
Between their loved homes and the war's desolation.
Blest with vict'ry and peace, may the Heav'n rescued land
Praise the Power that hath made and preserved us a nation!
Then conquer we must, when our cause it is just,
And this be our motto: "In God is our trust."
And the star-spangled banner in triumph shall wave
O'er the land of the free and the home of the brave!

ACTIVITY
WRITE YOUR OWN ANTHEM

1. Think about the things or people that are very special and important to you. Maybe it's music or soccer, or your pet or your grandmother. Choose one of these to write about.

2. Find a picture of that special person or thing, or something else that reminds you of it.

3. On a piece of paper, write down all the words that come to mind when you think of this person or thing. Include words that show how you feel as well as the images that come to your mind.

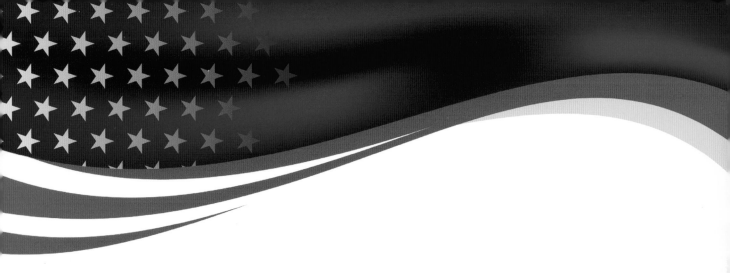

4. Once you have a list of about ten to twenty words, try to put them together in sentences or short phrases. Before you know it, you'll have your very own anthem. You can even try setting it to music!

LEARN MORE

Books

Kulling, Monica. *Francis Scott Key's Star-Spangled Banner*. New York, NY: Random House, 2012.

Monroe, Tyler, and Gail Saunders-Smith. *The Star-Spangled Banner*. North Mankato, MN: Capstone Press, 2013.

Nelson, Maria. *The National Anthem*. New York, NY: Gareth Stevens, 2015.

Websites

National Park Service: War of 1812
www.nps.gov/subjects/warof1812/for-kids.htm
The official site of the National Park Service, with information about historical sites of the War of 1812.

Smithsoniam: The Star-Spangled Banner
amhistory.si.edu/starspangledbanner
The official site of the Star-Spangled Banner.

INDEX

Baltimore, Battle of, 6, 7
garrison flag, 8
Key, Francis Scott, 7, 8, 12–14, 16
McHenry, Fort, 6, 7, 8, 10, 14

Pickersgill, Mary, 10
Smithsonian Institution, 10
Sousa, John Phillip, 17–18
"Star-Spangled Banner," compostion of, 7, 14

Super Bowl, 18
US flag, makers of, 10
US Flag Code, 18–19
War of 1812, 5

Published in 2017 by Enslow Publishing, LLC.
101 W. 23rd Street, Suite 240, New York, NY 10011

Library of Congress Cataloging-in-Publication Data
Names: Brannon, Cecelia H., author.
Title: Zoom in on the national anthem / Cecelia H. Brannon.
Description: New York, NY : Enslow Publishing, 2017. | Series: Zoom in on American symbols | Includes bibliographical references and index.
Identifiers: LCCN 2016021421| ISBN 9780766084483 (library bound) | ISBN 9780766084469 (pbk.) | ISBN 9780766084476 (6-pack)
Subjects: LCSH: Baltimore, Battle of, Baltimore, Md., 1814—Juvenile literature. | Star spangled banner (Song)—Juvenile literature. | United States—History—War of 1812—Flags—Juvenile literature. | National songs—United States—History and criticism—Juvenile literature. | Key, Francis Scott, 1779–1843—Juvenile literature. | Flags—United States—History—19th century—Juvenile literature.
Classification: LCC E356.B2 B73 2017 | DDC 929.9/20973—dc23
LC record available at https://lccn.loc.gov/2016021421

Printed in China

To Our Readers: We have done our best to make sure all website addresses in this book were active and appropriate when we went to press. However, the author and the publisher have no control over and assume no liability for the material available on those websites or on any websites they may link to. Any comments or suggestions can be sent by e-mail to customerservice@enslow.com.

Photo Credits: Cover, p. 1 (inset) Ron Vesely/Major League Baseball/Getty Images; cover, p. 1 (background flag) Stillfx/Shutterstock.com; pp. 4, 9, 11 Bettmann/Getty Images; p. 7 Greg Pease/Photographer's Choice/Getty Images; pp. 13, 17 Library of Congress Prints and Photographs Division; p. 15 Jon Bilous/Shutterstock.com; p. 19 Kevin Mazur/WireImage/Getty Images; p. 20 Tetra Images/Getty Images.
Interior pages graphic elements amtitus/DigitalVision Vectors/Getty Images (flag page borders), funnybank/DigitalVision Vectors/Getty Images (flag in circle), hvostik/Shutterstock.com (hand over heart).